I Am Enough

I Am Enough

Self-Reflection and Motivation for Women and Young Ladies

By: Dr. Shanelle Fields, LPC

2021 "I Am Enough"

Copyright © 2021 All rights reserved

All rights reserved. No part of this publication may be reproduced, stored in or introduced into a retrieval system, or transmitted in any form or by any means -- electronic, mechanical, photocopying, recording, or otherwise – except for brief quotations in printed reviews, without prior written permission from the publisher.
ISBN 978-1-7358268-8-2

For more information on the content of this book, email takingthe1ststep31@gmail.com

JMPinckney Publishing Company, LLC
104 Berkeley Square Lane
PMB 28
Goose Creek, South Carolina 29445

Cover Design: Manish Pathak
First printing June 2021 / Printed in the United States of America

Dedication

This book is dedicated to every woman or young lady who has ever been bullied, criticized, humiliated, cast aside, looked over, or been made to feel inadequate. You are unique. No one else could ever be you. So, wear your hurt proudly and use it as your motivation to love every part of you because YOU ARE ENOUGH!

Inspiration

I owe a large part of my success to my son, Isaiah. We grew up together. I always worked with other people's children in the educational world, but I could give them back. He was my child, and I couldn't give him back. I wanted to love and nurture him. I came to the realization that I needed to be the best version of myself to be the best mother I could for him. As a single mother, I wanted to defy the odds and raise him in a loving, communicative, high achieving, affectionate, and positive household. I wanted and still want great things for him. So, I had to be the example. Isaiah, you are my inspiration because you let me know daily and often that you love me and are proud of your mother. I recognized I needed to be Enough, so he could see what Enough was. I affirm him daily and often and tell him thank you for being my son. I am the most blessed mother in the world because I have you. Thank you for changing my life!

I am Enough

Dear Amazing Woman or Young Lady,

Hey you! Yes, the person reading this book that's upset, emotional, broken, tired, depressed, overwhelmed, anxious, unsure, apprehensive, and just feeling down about yourself. If you are reading this book, you may be feeling a little inadequate and less than your best. Let me tell you a little secret.... You are absolutely WORTH IT!

All of us have felt this way at some point in our lives. Whether you are a young lady who doesn't see the beauty staring back at you in the mirror or a woman who isn't quite where you desire to be in life, and You still MATTER! Maybe you are that female who may possess a few battle wounds because life hasn't been so kind to you. Let me reassure you, every one of us have been unhappy with who we are and where we are. You are in great company. I am here to help encourage and motivate you to acknowledge the place you are in, examine what's wrong, believe in yourself, and move to a positive place. Come and go with me on this journey of self-love and purpose. It is already inside of you but you just haven't recognized your potential or maybe you have lost sight of it along the way. Self-discovery is often a difficult journey, but a journey that will change your whole life. Be open to embracing and loving who you are despite your past. It does not define your present or your future.

Looking for the best in you,
Dr. Shanelle

Dr. Shanelle Fields, LPC

Before we get started, take a few minutes and truly think about yourself. How do you feel about who you are on the inside and the outside? Are you unhappy with how you look? Do you feel less than or inadequate? Feelings don't always register in words, so let's examine your self-esteem in numbers. Complete the Rosenberg Self-Esteem Scale below and compute your score. This number allows you to gauge whether or not your self-image is positive or negative. It doesn't matter the level of your self-esteem, you can always love yourself more.

Rosenberg Self-Esteem Scale

	STRONGLY DISAGREE	DISAGREE	AGREE	STRONGLY AGREE
I feel that I am a person of worth, at least on an equal plane with others.	○	○	○	○
I feel that I have a number of good qualities.	○	○	○	○
All in all, I am inclined to feel that I am a failure.	○	○	○	○
I am able to do things as well as most other people.	○	○	○	○
I feel I do not have much to be proud of.	○	○	○	○
I take a positive attitude toward myself.	○	○	○	○
On the whole, I am satisfied with myself.	○	○	○	○
I wish I could have more respect for myself.	○	○	○	○
I certainly feel useless at times.	○	○	○	○

Rosenberg, Morris. "Rosenberg Self-Esteem Scale." Self Report Measures for Love and Compassion Research: Self-Esteem, Fetzer

Institute,2000,fetzer.org/sites/default/files/images/stories/pdf/selfmeasures/Self_Measures_for_Self-Esteem_ROSENBERG_SELF-ESTEEM.pdf.

Scoring: Items 2, 5, 6, 8, and 9 are reverse scored. Give "Strongly Disagree" 1 point, "Disagree" 2 points, "Agree" 3 points, and "Strongly Agree" 4 points. Sum scores for all ten items. Keep scores on a continuous scale. Higher scores indicate higher self-esteem. The scale ranges from 0-30. Scores between 15 and 25 are within normal range; scores below 15 suggest low self-esteem.

What is your score? : _____

Instead of beating yourself up or getting down about how you feel, do something to change it. How can I do that? I have made so many mistakes and life hasn't been kind to me. I guess I don't like who I have become…That's alright. We all have something we have to work on. Self-love is the most important part of who we are; however, to alter or change behaviors, thoughts, and/or beliefs, we have to figure out where it came from and acknowledge the hurt. Once we fully accept that things aren't great and we aren't in a good place, the healing process can begin. Let's acknowledge that all is not well.

It's Ok Not to Be Ok

When you look in the mirror, who do you see? Are you smiling at the eyes, nose, lips, and hair that are attached to your face? Women tend to look at themselves in the mirror and pick out all the things that aren't right about us. Do you feel like something is missing? Maybe you are seeing your representative in the mirror. You know, that person the world sees. This is the mask you wear on the outside which covers the hurt and pain you may feel on the inside. So many women, old and young, smile on the outside but feel broken down, heavy, and tired on the inside. I don't want to leave out the young ladies. Maybe your mask is a result of not being popular or not feeling pretty enough or smart enough or enough of anything to just love you and know that you are beautiful just the way you are. Let's face it! This world and society can be so cruel. We compare ourselves to Instagram models, Facebook posts, magazine covers, fitness gurus, and our neighbors next door. Guess what? They aren't you. We forget to highlight the most positive things. What about you surviving that breakup, or not getting the promotion you have worked so hard for, or patting yourself on the back for standing your ground even though it wasn't the popular thing to do? Aren't those things noteworthy? I know you are probably reading these words saying I am not feeling any better. I hope this little jewel makes you feel a little bit better. It is ok to not be ok.

Sometimes, we have to live in this existence of not being our best selves. We hear so many preconceived notions about women being strong and being able to handle everything. Well, sometimes you can't handle everything and the strong tower comes crashing down. Maybe that's how you are feeling right now. All of the things you are carrying have all of a sudden become too heavy for you. At this very moment, please place all of your bags down and rest for just a moment. Put down the Superwoman cape, put down the doting Mom and wife cape, put down the industrious employee or employer role, put down the struggling small business owner hat, put down the loving friend who solves everyone's problems, put down the appearance of the student that has it all together, and just be (fill in the blank with your name). Breathe out all of the roles, titles, jobs, requirements, and aspirations, and breathe in Love of Self.

Those bags that you have been carrying have overtaken who you are. We didn't even speak of the bags you carry from your past. We have bags that are filled with trauma, grief, pain, insecurity, low self-esteem, defeat, and just not being enough. Even though most people won't say it's ok to live in this space, sometimes you have to exist in not being ok. Believe it or not, many of us know how to exist in all of this stuff. It is how we have learned to function. It's almost like they have become attached to us. They appear in our thoughts when we are alone and cause us to think that we aren't capable of being all that we can be. One of the ways to begin the process of self-love is to do a self-reflection. Yes, you have to look at yourself even if you don't want to. Let me help you make this process a little easier. Pull out your mirror or walk to your nearest bathroom or even take out your cell phone and turn the camera into a selfie. Look at yourself in the mirror for at least 1 minute, uninterrupted. Recall all of your experiences, good and bad. Take a minute and process how you got to this place feeling so bad about yourself. Is it because you were never validated or approved as a child? Maybe you looked for solace or friendship in someone who didn't reciprocate your loyalty. It could also be you are at a crossroads in your life because you haven't gotten to the place you thought you would be at this very moment. Regardless of the mistake, setback, downfall, mishap, ridicule, humiliation, and or defeat, you can still love who you are, flaws and all. Here is another little piece of advice to let you know you are in good company. Everyone has something to deal with. Her problem is not the same as your problem, but it still holds both of you back from acknowledging all the greatness inside of you.

Think about all of those bags you are carrying and write them down in the circles (bags) on this page. Give each of your bags a label. While you are writing these weights down, bring to your mind how this has affected who you are. I have given you a couple of examples.

I am Enough

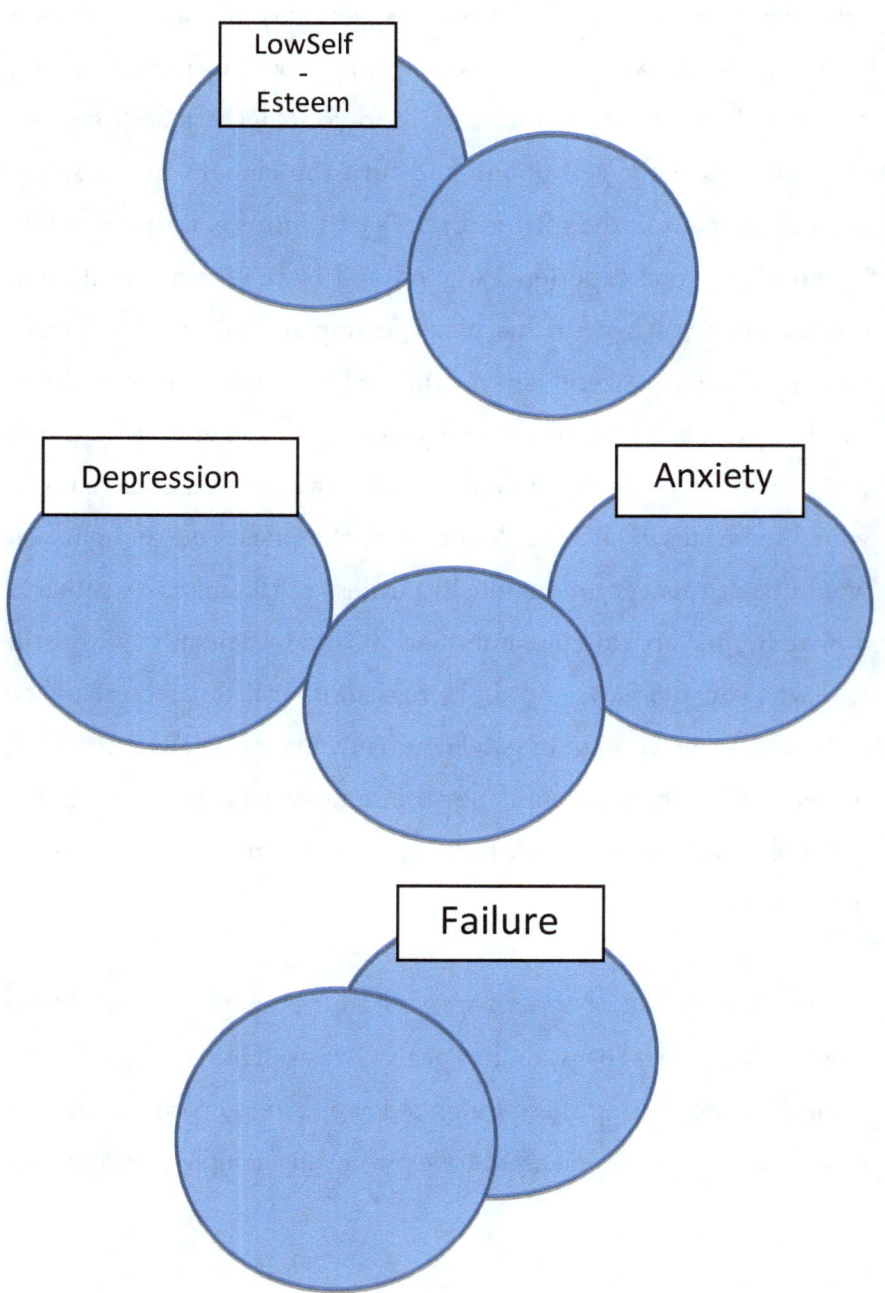

What Kind of Bags are You Carrying?

Did it feel good to unload all of those things? You have been existing in all of this "stuff" for a long time. Completing this activity may have been difficult for you to do for many different reasons. This process allowed you to be in the moment, not focusing on what didn't get done today, what you have to do tomorrow, or what someone else needs. Just in case you have forgotten... You are very important! To begin to love yourself, you must understand and be comfortable knowing that something is wrong. Many women of all ages beat themselves up daily for not being in a positive place. Unfortunately, the strong tower is who we desire to be, but in all actuality, we have so many things weighing us down that our inner selves hardly have a chance to surface.

I am giving you permission right now to release the wall that you have built up around yourself. I am giving you permission to release that emotion that you hold in. Release those tears that only come in small doses because you don't want anyone to see them. Release that anger for the person who you let in and he/she hurt you. Release that vision of the person you desire to be but haven't quite gotten there yet. Release that yell for the person that didn't recognize your purpose and allow you to use your gift. Release each thing that is holding you back from being your best self! Go ahead and release! (Insert EMOTIONAL RELEASE HERE). This means to cry, yell, scream, or moan; that's right. It is a great thing to let go of the tension that keeps you held down and unhappy. LET IT ALL GO! Wasn't that a good feeling? Have you gotten it out of your system? Release as often and as much as you need. This makes room for positive memories and ideas. I am so glad that you finally realized you weren't in a good place and know why you have just been existing. Let's examine what you have been feeling because you may honestly think that's how life is supposed to be. Guess what? You DESERVE MORE!

Acknowledging What You Feel

I hope the beginning of this book didn't turn you away but allowed you to look at your pain and understand why you have so many reservations about yourself. Each situation, circumstance, experience, and choice shape our perspective about life. Sometimes, the result is positive and we are ecstatic about the next steps; however, the end results can also make us apprehensive, hesitant, guarded, and fearful. These results can also leave scars that take time to heal. After releasing those bags you have been carrying, I hope you feel lighter and better. If weight has been lifted off of your shoulders, it is important to examine what you were feeling. How can you move forward or even prepare for the next wave of emotions if you don't acknowledge what you feel? Take a few minutes and bring back to your mind all of the things that went through your head. Were you angry at others who hurt you or didn't engage in your vision? Did you feel ashamed because the choice you made didn't turn out favorably for you? Maybe that person you had strong feelings for really hurt you and made you feel inadequate. These memories may be really painful for you to envision but necessary to recount to better understand your feelings.

I am Enough

Hurt can be defined in so many ways. For some, hurt is a physical feeling that actually causes aching in your heart. Pain can also cause intense anger and negative reactions. Hurt has also been known to bring tears. This is an outward physical release of an inward emotion. Guess what? Emotional release is a great thing! Cry, yell, scream say a few bad words if you need to. Air your grievances. It is more detrimental to keep them bottled up inside of you. You don't have to necessarily say them to anyone. These emotions are about you. Hurt and pain that is not resolved begin to weigh on you. Of course, your mental and emotional mind are heavy, but your physical is affected as well. Deep sadness, guilt, trauma, shame, grief, and low self-esteem alter your daily living. Activities that used to be fun become a chore to do. Sometimes it is even hard to get out of bed and begin your day. Your thoughts are often overwhelmingly negative. How is low self-esteem challenged or broken? It takes reframing and turning negative thoughts into positive ones. If you have ever felt as if you didn't matter or no one needed you, I am here to reassure you that your presence is very much needed in this world. Your purpose may not have surfaced yet or you are just trying to figure it out. Despite feeling low and undervalued, your worth is still great. Let's work on finding the best parts of you and focusing on all the positive things that make you special.

Power of Positive Affirmation

An affirmation is a strong statement or sentiment that expresses a positive thought. It is important to subscribe to positive thoughts when trying to break negative ideas. In the counseling world, we contribute positive affirmations to Cognitive Behavioral Therapy. Essentially, this type of therapy focuses on changing negative thought processes and harmful stereotypes. If someone is told he or she is unattractive repeatedly, this pervasive negative thought becomes a normal idea and way of life. In essence, the person now believes he or she is unattractive, even if that is not an idea ever thought about before. Have you ever experienced this feeling? It is amazing how quickly our minds can adjust and hold on to the opinions of others and attach the label to ourselves.

Positive affirmations help fight and break negative stereotypes. Ladies, this means your failed relationship, lost job, major mistake, or bad choice doesn't define who you are. This means you have the opportunity to change your life one positive thought at a time. Even if you weren't chosen to be the star in the play, his or her girlfriend, the class president, the MVP of the team, or the person that wasn't chosen for the scholarship, your defining moment does not rest with these outcomes. Your defining moment comes when you realize you are still VALUABLE! That's right. You have worth. Here is another little jewel for you to remember. Your VALUE increases when you recognize your WORTH. Let me say it again. Your VALUE increases when you recognize your WORTH. **You are important! You are needed! You are valuable!** These important words are bold because they mean such a great deal. They are reminders of the great significance you hold and are examples of positive affirmations. One of the ways I help build self-esteem in therapy is to have clients create a positive affirmation. One of my favorites is "I Deserve Good Things!" The thing about change is that sometimes we need to see it written in plain view often, daily, and much. We also need to hear it said out loud as a reminder that we are dynamic and powerful people.

In addition to positive affirmations, positive "I" statements also evoke change. These are strong bold assertions or strong positive statements about you as a person. Sometimes, putting ownership in front of our most positive characteristics reminds us, women, that we are a force to be reckoned with. The next time you are confronted with a difficult situation, reframe your mind with a positive "I" statement. For example, work or school has become overwhelming and the tasks being asked of you seem unattainable, and you feel insecure about your skills and capabilities. At your desk in school or at work, whisper to yourself, "I am capable of great things." No one has to know what you are thinking or saying. These powerful words are a reassurance that you can accomplish anything. It also breaks the negative thoughts of being incapable of handling difficult tasks. Do you need a reminder of how awesome you are? Situations and experiences often make us feel inadequate, especially if the outcome was not favorable or positive. Creating a positive "I" statement helps reframe your automatic response to think negatively about yourself. It may be difficult and even feel weird to list or think about your positive attributes. Here is some food for thought. If you can't identify positive traits about yourself, how do you expect anyone else to see them in you? It is not arrogant or boastful to recognize the best parts of you. Remembering the good things assists us in feeling good about ourselves, even when situations and people make us feel otherwise. Now, it's your turn to practice this skill. It may take a little time to think of all the great things you have to offer, but if you realize all the greatness in you, I am sure you can put something down. To aid you in finding your positives, I will offer examples on the next page.

Examples of Positive "I Statements

I Am Beautiful.

                                            I Am Confident.

I Am Compassionate.

                                            I Am Worthy of Love.

I Am Capable of Endless Possibilities.

                    I Am Able to Create Success for Myself.

I Am Strong.

                                            I Am Loved.

                    I Am Worthy of Healing.

I Am Alive.

I am Enough

Take a moment and think about all the things you do well, even if your mood is not happy or you feel like a failure. This activity is not meant to be completed all at once, but it does require you to be a little boastful about yourself and list some of your best qualities. Go ahead and fill in these blanks with positive and bold statements about who you are! Yes, you! You can do it. I believe in you! One more thing, while you are thinking about all the great things that are inside of you, create a strong bold positive affirmation that will help you push through the difficult days. This mantra is your motivator on bad days and when things don't quite work out the way you want them to. This statement is a reminder that your future is bright.

My strong positive affirmation is: _____

_____
_____
_____
_____
_____
_____

I Am _____.

I Am _____.

I Am _____.

I Am _____.

I Am _____.

I Am _____.

I Am _____.

I Am _____.

I Am _____.

I Am _____.

I Am _____.

Did it feel good to think about and acknowledge all of the great things you have to offer or can obtain? There are endless possibilities to what you can accomplish. One of your priorities should be to love yourself unconditionally. That should be #1. If you don't love yourself, no one else will. Self-love is an inside job, and it takes constant upliftment and positive reminders. Once you have completed this activity, pick your strongest and most endearing affirmation and post it somewhere you can see it. It can be written on a simple piece of paper or a sticky note. Every single day, look in the mirror or on your desk and remember to say your affirmation. These strong words may start as a whisper but saying them often and believing in the power of your words will help them become loud, strong, and proud. Once these words have

I am Enough

become a constant in your life, you will begin to see how much your value has increased and how good you feel about yourself. You will begin to carry yourself more confidently and believe in your ability to do great things. The idea is to transform your mind into thinking You Are Enough! Sometimes we are own worst critics. Now, it's time to be your biggest fan because no one can be you better than YOU!

Your Inner Circle

In this process of rebuilding and transformation, there is one important piece of information we often forget about. Despite this change being about you, it is important to remember who you are attached to. Those closest to you transfer their energy, good or bad, into your personal space. Is your closest confidant a part of your process? Is your best friend cheering you on and sharing in your pain? Believe it or not, the people closest to us can affect the process of loving ourselves more. Wait a minute…. You mean my best friend or family plays a role in my healing? Yes, they do. How do they affect my process? Everyone connected to you makes a deposit or withdrawal into your life.

Issues with mental health have not always received attention. This means everyone will not subscribe or believe in the metamorphosis of being your best self. Some people actually believe low self-esteem is a fad that will go away in time. They are partially correct. Low self-esteem can be amended in time with proper emotional self-reflection, deep understanding, and changes in negative belief systems. Your family member could be experiencing the same thing you are and never acknowledge the way it has affected him/her. One of the things I constantly affirm in therapy is to surround yourself with positive people! It doesn't matter if the two of you have been friends for many years or you have been close since elementary school and were in the same classes growing up. Miserable and unhappy people often enjoy the company of others. These types of people will keep you in a stuck place. It is very difficult to progress and move forward if the energy around you is negative. The people closest to you can have a hand in depleting your happiness or replenishing your positivity. Believe it or not, our inner circle affects what and how we think about ourselves. In essence, we value their opinions about our lives; however, their thoughts don't have to be included in your process. Encouragement and support are two of the greatest gifts someone attached to you can give, and it doesn't cost a dime. Make sure the people closest to you are radiating positivity and light.

Self-Care is a Necessity, Not an Inconvenience

I am sure you have been hearing the word "self-care" used a lot lately and you may be wondering what exactly it is. Self-care is an activity or activities that are focused solely on YOU. It is not piling other things on top of an already full plate. It is not agreeing to take on another work project, chair a committee, be the President of this group at school, incorporate the next business, or watch someone else's child or children. It is ok to say NO when self-care is needed. Self-care means meeting the immediate needs of the one person who is tired, overwhelmed, burnt out, stressed, depressed, feeling inadequate, overworked, underpaid, exhausted, anxious, and filled to the brim with stuff.

Self-care is not a difficult thing to do. Self-care often means to stop doing everything; however, the stopping of everything sometimes means we have to focus on what isn't working for us and how we aren't happy in the current state we are in, which takes us back to self-reflection and assessment. For the young ladies, this may mean putting down the cell phone and not answering every text or looking at every notification. Business owners may have to close up shop for a day or two just to recuperate and relax to be able to open the doors again. You see, living well takes effort. In many instances, this action requires giving every piece of energy you have to make it work. Caring for oneself is just the opposite. It means meeting your needs in one simple way. You don't do anything. Downtime is not a bad thing, even for ambitious and determined women. This is how you replenish all that you have been and are pouring out every day. As women, our identities are often tied to the roles we play; this point was discussed in the first part of the book; however, it still rings true here. Maybe you are a caretaker for elderly parents or younger siblings, and your day consists of school or work and tending to the needs of others. Are your needs not important? What about the single mother who has all the responsibility of her household on her shoulders? Do you know how much stress a working mother carries? Being a wife or significant other, mother, employer, employee, captain of the cheerleading squad, National Honor Society treasurer, Dean's List student, travel softball player, entrepreneur, stylist, and even a secretary all require large amounts of focus, attention, effort, and dedication. Let's face it. These jobs become our whole lives, and we forget who the person is attached to the roles we play. Our names are now, So and So, Real Estate Agent, the High School Booster Club's Vice President, Executive Director of Human Resources, or Student Body President. What happened to just being (insert your name here)? Yes, we work hard for these roles, but how do we decompress and release? Self-care is one of the ways we can keep going. It also reminds you of your importance and value. If you don't value yourself, no one else will. Of course, I have practice for you but not without some examples.

Self-Care Is.........

Self-care is a long hot bubble bath without technology or anyone else present. It is just you, your thoughts, and the bubbles. Be sure to stay in there until you see wrinkles... (Lol)

Self-care is a long walk in the park, your subdivision, your school's track, or around your neighborhood. This is a great time to listen to inspirational music.

Self-care is sitting, playing, or laying near a body of water. The movement of water brings about a sense of calm.

Self-care is turning on your favorite podcast or motivational speaker for inspiration before starting your day, whether you are going to work or school.

Self-care is reading a good book or one of those grocery store magazines, all by yourself. It's nice to see what other people are doing.

Self-care is having your favorite meal; it doesn't matter if it's home cooked or restaurant brought.

I am Enough

Self-care is reciting your positive affirmations and Positive I Am Statements every day until you believe them.

Self-care is smiling when you see that beautiful woman or young lady in front of you and realizing she is worthy of great things. (This is a purposeful intentional practice that hopefully gets the woman to love who she sees staring back at her.)

Self-care is going to the place or space where you feel the most at peace, safe, and loved.

Self-care is putting on your favorite outfit or piece of jewelry, just because it makes you feel good.

Self-care is taking a selfie every day of the week and loving the person staring back at you!

These are just a few examples of what loving yourself looks like. A nap could be self-care for someone who is always on the go. You are probably saying these things don't seem to be difficult to do, and they aren't; however, the hard part is in realizing you have been neglecting the #1 person who needs it, and that's you. The other hard part is making self-care a continuous and intentional part of your life because Self-Care is a Necessity, Not an Inconvenience.

Here is a place to write down your self-care thoughts and rituals. These things are about you and what makes you happy.

My Daily Self-Care Is.........

_____
_____
_____
_____
_____
_____
_____
_____

My Weekly Self-Care Is......

_____
_____
_____
_____
_____
_____
_____
_____

I am Enough

My Monthly Self-Care Is……..

_____

_____

_____

_____

_____

_____

_____

Dr. Shanelle Fields, LPC

Dear Beautiful Lady,

I hope this book was helpful and lifted your spirit. I aimed to bring a little sparkle and light into your life that has been missing. Maybe you have forgotten how amazing you are. These exercises are just a few of the very simple ways I work with clients on building self-esteem, and I believe they can assist you in finding the best version of yourself. If you wonder why you saw the words "you" and "us" throughout this book, it's because I am talking to myself, as I speak to you. We all get down and feel heavy with everything on our shoulders. But...we don't have to live like this. What you were doing before is merely existing and not living. Don't you want to LIVE? (Learning through Independent Varied Experiences). Enjoying life very much rests with the way you see things. Is your view half empty or half full?

Remember you are a force to be reckoned with and deserve every great thing that is coming your way. Self-esteem affects every aspect of our lives, and it governs how we live. If you are hesitant and apprehensive, it may hold you back from being all you can be. I hope you are working to change your view to a positive one.

Thank you for taking this journey with me. The person reading this closing letter should be moving from Broken to Healed, from Inadequate to Qualified, and from Fearful to Courageous. All of these strong positive qualities are already present inside of you. You just needed a little help pulling them out. Continue to fall more in love with yourself every day because YOU ARE ENOUGH!

From One Victorious Woman to Another,
Dr. Shanelle

Acknowledgments

I would like to take a moment to acknowledge all of the special people in my life. God is my source of strength and my everything. Without Him, I am nothing. To my son, Isaiah, I am so grateful to be your mother. You have given me so much and increased my desire to be more so that I can be a great paradigm for you. To my father, my coach and #1 fan, you were my first example of love from a man, and you spoiled me rotten and still do. My younger brother is my protector and 2nd father, or so he thinks. He is always looking over my shoulder and reminding me to be the best version of myself. My mother was my best friend, and I miss her, but she was the best example of a lady. I find myself growing to be more and more like her every day. To my family and friends, thank you for always encouraging me to live out my dreams and accepting me for who I am. Thank you to a special friend for reminding me of what I deserve.

To the 10-year-old little girl, the outspoken but broken teenager, the smart and hardworking but insecure young adult, and the ashamed 30-year-old mother, YOU HAVE BEEN AND WILL ALWAYS BE ENOUGH!

Reference

Rosenberg, Morris. "Rosenberg Self-Esteem Scale." Self Report Measures for Love and

Compassion Research: Self-Esteem, Fetzer Institute, 2000,

Fetzer.org/sites/default/files/images/stories/pdf/selfmeasures/Self_Measures_

For_Self-Esteem_ROSENBERG_SELF-ESTEEM.pdf

About The Author

Dr. Shanelle Fields is a native of Florence, South Carolina. Her education includes a BA in English Education from the College of Charleston, a Masters in School Counseling from the Citadel Military College, and a Ph.D. in Human Services and Counseling from Capella University. For the last 18 years, she has been a middle and high school English teacher and a Professional School Counselor.

In November 2018, she completed her supervision to become an LPC and has opened a private practice in Summerville, SC. Dr. Shanelle works to help others who are struggling with self-esteem, grief, anxiety, depression, and women's issues. Due to her love of education and counseling, she has given many presentations, speeches, and motivational messages to encourage others. Her proudest accomplishment is raising her now 10-year-old son as a single parent, working full-time, and completing her doctorate. Dr. Fields knows what it is to be in a "stuck place."

Her mottos are "Every day you have the chance to change two people's lives, yours and someone else's and to always remember You Are Enough. Her practice website is www.takingthefirststep.net

www.ingramcontent.com/pod-product-compliance
Lightning Source LLC
Chambersburg PA
CBHW062207100526
44589CB00014B/2001